FINDING
Peace

DR. REBECCA I. PAYNE

authorHOUSE®

AuthorHouse™
1663 Liberty Drive
Bloomington, IN 47403
www.authorhouse.com
Phone: 833-262-8899

Published by AuthorHouse 07/14/2023

ISBN: 979-8-8230-1152-5 (sc)
ISBN: 979-8-8230-1151-8 (e)

Library of Congress Control Number: 2023913021

Print information available on the last page.

Any people depicted in stock imagery provided by Getty Images are models, and such images are being used for illustrative purposes only.
Certain stock imagery © Getty Images.

Scripture quotations are taken from the New American Standard Bible®, Copyright © 1960, 1962, 1963, 1968, 1971, 1972, 1973, 1975, 1977, 1995 by The Lockman Foundation. Used by permission.

This book is printed on acid-free paper.

You have instructed me and taught me
in the way which I should go;
You have advised me with Your eye upon me.

CONTENTS

CHAPTER 1

In the Beginning

Though the lessons have been many, it's often the simple things that endure.

I used to sit and marvel at the people who sat on the porch quietly rocking in their chairs, not speaking, just looking at the passersby or the clouds in the sky. They used to have such profound words of wisdom when they did speak, such awe-inspiring words, such captivating stories. I used to love to sit with them and marvel at their stories, never wanting to leave, always wanting to come back.

Miss Mazey is one such "porch person". She's 82 years young and so full of life and so full of the Word. She's a beautiful soul with crisp white hair and piercing brown eyes; eyes that make you feel she sees in and through you. Her skin is bronze and so very smooth with nary a wrinkle, just smile lines because of her warm perpetual smile. She doesn't look 82 years at all but seems so much younger!

There is rarely a day I see Miss Mazey that she doesn't greet me with her dimpled grin and playfulness.

She has a mother figure, neither plump nor overly thin. Even though she was married, a soul she has since laid to rest, and has raised five children and countless nieces and nephews, we still call her Miss Mazey out of deference to her age and wisdom. She's everyone's mother. She's my spiritual mother, my prayer partner, and my friend.

I met Miss Mazey at a time in my life when I was getting to know God but not totally committed to following Jesus. I had accepted Jesus as my Savior, and had been baptized, but wasn't obeying all of the commands. I wasn't living a committed Christian life. I was also judgmental.

One day I was at a birthday party for Miss Mazey's daughter. I had never met Miss Mazey but had heard wonderful stories from her daughter Gloria about her.

When I met Miss Mazey, an odd feeling came over me. It was like I had known her my whole life and I needed to reconnect with her. She looked at me intently and later told me she had the same feeling. It was God who brought us together and we both knew it. Immediately she asked for my number. She gave me her number and her address and told me to connect with her.

We began a fast friendship. She immediately felt like a mother to me but also so much more. Over time we grew very close, often talking about life and our relationship with God. I'd never met anyone like her who not only understood the Bible but how it relates to everyday living. More specifically, she helped me see how God was moving in my life if I'd only listen to Him and read His word.

I'd call Miss Mazey or go see her. We'd talk for long hours about God and the goings on in my life and hers. She'd counsel me with wisdom, reminding me that God's Holy Spirit was working in me to cleanse, make me whole, sanctify, and give me peace. All I needed to do was heed God's wisdom and obey Him.

Miss Mazey spent many a time counseling me on peace and quiet time and slowing down. That elusive time that we strive for after we've run around all day trying to be that super-woman or super-man. Funny how we can climb the ladder of success, work hard all week and play harder all weekend, but not make time to just be still even though we claim we want a moment's rest.

Miss Mazey revealed our lifestyles don't make room for quiet time but making time to still ourselves is something we must actively do. It goes against everything our nature is. We are action-oriented, strivers. We are always busy. We don't sit still. We are active and anything that is not active, in our minds, is not alive.

But through all this activity we are tired. We don't get enough rest, much less sleep. Our bodies are crying out for a time to just sit and be. We want time to be alone, have time not to think, and time to relish in the quiet.

Miss Mazey told me, "Don't you know God made time for this? God rested on the seventh day (Genesis 2.2) and so can you. God wants you to rest and refresh yourself for He knows what's best for you. But you've got to want it. You've got to make time for time." I started paying more attention to my quiet time.

One day I was sitting on the porch with Miss Mazey, and she asked me, "How often do you sit and count your blessings? Do you have anything you're hoping for? What about your quiet time? Do you take the time to just sit still and look out at the sky and wonder at God?"

I was so overwhelmed by her barrage of questions, not knowing where to start to answer. I thought in line with these questions every day but didn't have the answers. That Miss Mazey asked these seemingly innocent questions now was important. I knew they would lead me on a journey I was afraid to take. I couldn't catch my breath.

"Hold on Miss Mazey! One question at a time!" I laughed.

"Well, Jamie, do you count your blessings?" she squealed with laughter.

"Not often enough!" I said sobering a bit.

"How do you know how good you have it? If you don't count them every day, you'll miss opportunities to praise God. Don't wait until you lose what you have! Miss Mazey said.

"Seems to me it's hard to realize how good you've got it until you see someone who doesn't have it as good as you," I said. "I don't like to think about the darker side of life. I just want to live peaceably and go about my days in simplicity."

"That's just it," Miss Mazey said. "You've got to know that your life is good to realize the benefits of what you have. You've got to understand how it could have been so that you know how good you've got it. Don't be afraid to look at the goings on in life. Sometimes you have to read the news to know just how good your life is and to pray for those who are not as fortunate as you. Your Bible teaches this. It tells us to count our blessings, to remember all God has done for us."

Miss Mazey sighed reflectively and continued, "Genesis 9.15 reminds us, 'and I will remember My covenant, which is between Me and you and every living creature of all flesh; and never again shall the water become a flood to destroy all flesh.' God reminded Noah and every creature on Earth He would not destroy the Earth again. In Exodus, God heard the groanings of the Israelites, and 'So God heard their groaning; and God remembered His covenant with Abraham, Isaac, and Jacob,' (Exodus 2.24).

God will always remember you and wants you to remember all He's done for you and all He will do for you. The Apostle Paul reminds us, 'remember that you were at that time separate from Christ, excluded from the commonwealth of Israel, and strangers to the covenants of promise, having no hope and without God in the world' (Ephesians 2.12).

It's important to remember where you come from and how far you came to be where you are now. Take the time to reflect and be grateful for all that you have."

I sighed with the knowledge that I had been given a great lesson, thinking this was all Miss Mazey would speak about, but she continued.

"Are you reading your Bible every day?"

"Well, almost every day!" I said thoughtfully. Miss Mazey had counseled me that it wasn't enough to pray but that you had to read the Bible every day to get to know God.

"Well, if you're reading almost every day how do you not know how good you've got it?" Miss Mazey said with a mischievous grin.

I sighed shaking my head, knowing I'd been trapped. "You got me there! I guess I just never really think much about how good things are until I run into problems."

"That's the problem with your generation. You don't focus on the things that are important until something happens. That's why y'all are stressed out and tired all the time. You don't take time to count your blessings and to stop and be still once in a while."

I couldn't argue with her there.

"So, what are you hoping for?" Miss Mazey asked sheepishly. I could tell she was leading me just where she wanted me.

"Well, I guess I want to slow down, to relax more. I want to have peace in my life and to discover new things."

"How are you gonna have any of that if you don't have peace with God and you don't make time to rest?"

There it was. I had absolutely no answer. Anything I said after that would be useless, an excuse.

Miss Mazey knew she had me, so she just sat back, smoothed her slacks, crossed her feet, put her hands over her stomach, and looked out at the yard. A long time passed just listening to nature, looking at nothing in particular. I knew to be quiet. I knew she wanted me to digest all that was said, to reach the proper conclusion.

Nothing was going to change unless I changed it. The problem was I didn't know how to change and wasn't sure I wanted to. Yes, there were things I didn't like about my life, but I wasn't sure I wanted to invest the time in making it better or different.

Because we were sitting on the porch and because I didn't want to go down the road Miss Mazey was trying to take me on, I started turning over in my mind the wonder of God in His creation. It seemed the right direction to take in a conversation that was disturbing me because of the complexity I had created in my life. I wasn't ready to be honest with myself that the life I had I had created.

Finally, Miss Mazey said thoughtfully, "Creation gives insight into the intricacy, and the level of detail, God imparts to all He created. You are uniquely you. There is no one like you. And when He formed you in your mother's womb, He determined the path He wanted to put you on so that you would be successful and prosper in all that you desired to do. "Before I formed you in the womb I knew you," (Jeremiah 1.5). He even put the desires in your heart so that you would attempt to aspire to great things. 'Delight yourself in the Lord; And He will give you the desires of your heart' (Psalm 37.4)."

Miss Mazey looked deeply at me for a moment and then said, "God is telling you He has a plan for you, plans to prosper you and to help you grow. He wants to give you a life pleasing to Him, a life that encourages you, a life that leads you to encourage others. 'For I know the plans that I have for you,' declares the Lord, 'plans for welfare and not for calamity to give you a future and a hope' (Jeremiah 29.11)."

I looked down at my hands and said quietly, "I wonder what those plans are seeing everything seems hard right now."

Miss Mazey continued to look out at the garden. "You can have the desires of your heart once you learn that the things of this world are temporary. The things of God are eternal and enduring. 'Seek first the kingdom of God and all these things will be added to you' (Matthew 6.33). That is what He said and that is what He wants to do for you.

We struggle because we don't know what it means to be free. We don't often think of ourselves in terms of bondage, so we don't know how to ask God to help us break the yolk that this fallen world places on us. 'So also, we, while we were children, were held in bondage under the elemental things of the world' (Galatians 4.3). We don't think of Satan controlling and manipulating situations in our lives, but he does.

We are not free when we have addictions and when we are afflicted with disease, sickness, and mental health issues. We are under the subjection of any enemy of our soul when we can't agree and don't get along. But Christ Jesus can set us free from the bondage that locks away our souls. And with this freedom comes a desire to come closer to Him, to get to know Him deeper.

Nothing in life will prepare you for a Savior who can free you until you understand there is more to life than what you can see. Life on this earth is complicated by prescriptions we don't aspire to. Following the crowd won't get you to the places you want to go. You have to step out, in faith, believing the Creator of the universe cares for you and wants the best for you. 'So, if the Son makes you free, you will be free indeed' John 8.36)."

I nodded my head in agreement, remaining silent to take in what Miss Mazey was saying.

After a while of silence still focused her attention on the yard, Miss Mazey continued. "Understanding you are loved beyond measure and accepting that love is the first step to reconciling with

God. The next step is often harder; recognizing you are a sinner and need a savior. Acknowledging sin is the hardest thing you will ever have to do. But it gets easier from there."

"I've done that," I said smugly.

Knowing some parts of my story Miss Mazey said, "Keeping one foot in the world and one foot connected to the things of God won't work. Unfortunately, that's how most of us spend our lives. We don't seek kingdom things because we think we have to give up a lot. On the one hand, we have a lot to give up. Self-doubt, addictions, afflictions, poverty, low self-esteem, and disbelief. Only God knows the journey ahead of you when you decide to trust Him, believing in Him."

"Well, I believe in God. Not sure how much I trust Him though." I said more to myself than to Miss Mazey.

"Trust is a big step to take. Miss Mazey breathed. "It starts with the journey of belief. Believing God is and that He wants to have a relationship with you is pretty hard to understand. 'Trust in Him at all times, O people; Pour out your heart before Him; God is a refuge for us. (Psalm 62.8).'

"Why would the Creator want to spend time with me?" I asked softly, almost to myself, as if I was afraid of the answer.

I've struggled with this myself for quite some time, but when I finally just accepted the truth of God's love, everything began to fall into place, albeit slowly. God doesn't want to overwhelm you. He takes His time to introduce Himself to you, letting you get to know Him. The Bible was written over centuries, so it just makes sense that it takes time to get to know God and understand all His characteristics and desires."

"How did you get closer to God Miss Mazey?" I inquired, shifting in my chair.

"I spend time in the quiet and listening to creation. It helps to ease your frayed nerves. It takes the stress away and gives God time to let you hear His still, small voice. It also gives you time to hear yourself breathe, to take your mind off your worries, off all the things you have to do."

Reflecting for a moment, Miss Mazey went on to say, "I often find flower arranging to be soothing. Cutting the flowers and arranging them in a vase can be relaxing. Having the beauty around me adds to the peacefulness and quiets my troubled mind. I can look at beauty and ponder God's wonderful, delicate, intricate, handiwork. All it takes is a moment and the peace settles in, and I begin to rest."

"That sounds lovely," I said. "I might try that. At this point, anything would be helpful."

Miss Mazey looked at me for a moment and then said, "Whatever it is that calms your soul and lifts you to a curiosity about your Creator, that is what you are meant to do to set you on the path to peace. Notice I said it's a path to peace. This marks just the beginning of the journey.

Spending time in God's Word, letting Him lead you through the intricacies of what He said to the children of old, and what He wants you to glean from it now, takes time. The Word is a living, breathing, document and each time you read it, as you grow into studying it, you will be fascinated by how relevant it still is, and how many lessons you can glean from the pages. It's a conversation between you and God that never grows old."

I smiled a little thinking God gave me a blessing in Miss Mazey. She had a way of getting to the heart of the matter and imparting words of wisdom that remain embedded in your soul.

We sat looking out at nothing in particular, taking in the beauty of Miss Mazey's beautiful garden. I sighed, beginning to feel contentment and wondered at Miss Mazey's wisdom.

Miss Mazey folded her hands in her lap and started rocking in her chair. We stayed that way, in silence, for the rest of my visit.

CHAPTER 2

Why am I here?

One day as we were sitting on the porch, I asked Miss Mazey, "Have you ever wondered why you are here? Why were you born?"

Miss Mazey looked up at the sky, folded her hands in her lap, and just sighed. After a while, she said, "Part of the journey of self-discovery is learning who you can be and what you are meant to do. It's not so hard to discover as some might lead you to believe.

All sorts of self-help books say they will lead you to enlightenment, but true enlightenment comes when you understand the one who Created you has a plan for you in His great and grand design. He wants you to learn of Him so that He can impart the answers to the mysteries that plague your soul."

"I often ask myself, Why am I here?", I said softly.

Miss Mazey looked at me for a seemingly long time. Eventually, she broke the silence saying, "Jamie, you are part of a unique design meant to build you up as you build up others. You are an object of love and are meant to share love with others. That's it! That's the plan! The real question is how are you meant to do this? What tools are you meant to use to sustain yourself while you're on the planet? That's the part of life that involves work, making a living."

I thought about this for a while. I kept silent knowing Miss Mazey would continue her thought.

Miss Mazey sat reflecting for a moment then said, "Often, we pick jobs based on what society is interested in or what we see others doing. The truth is that we should each select to do work that interests us, bringing with it fascination and excitement. And when that excitement passes, we're meant to move on to the next assignment.

True, some things are not prosperous, and won't make a lot of money. That's why you get to do what you can while pursuing what you want to do. Your so-called calling will also kick in. It's that thing that God wants you to do and has gifted and anointed you to do."

I started thinking about what she said, and we let the silence pass amicably by.

After a time, Miss Mazey said looking intently at me, "Jamie, God never meant for work to be a drudgery. We've spent too much time killing our dreams for the sake of income and complaining there isn't enough time in the day to do the things we really want to do. This is such a cop-out! What we really mean is we're afraid that if we try to fulfill our dreams, we're afraid we won't succeed. We're afraid of failure. Failure is its own measure that leads to success. If you fall or fail, get right back up and try again!"

I nodded my head saying, "Over the years I've heard others say the same thing. I've said it too. But it's another thing to live it."

"Well, if we don't try, we spend years wishing we had tried, living with regret. We'll never know if that next try could have led to success. What most don't understand is that trying can lead to peace. Trying is its own reward that soothes the soul and gives the mind rest. 'One hand full of rest is better than two fists full of labor

11

and striving after wind' (Ecclesiastes 4.6). Note though that it is rest that leads to happiness and fullness of joy.

Look at Moses in the book Exodus. Many know the story of the parting of the Red Sea, but few have read the whole story in its entirety. Moses went before Pharoah many times over the span of many months before the Israelites were set free to leave Egypt. Each time he went to Pharoah telling him to let the Israelites go, Pharoah said no. Then God would send a plague. Moses returns to Pharoah and again asks that the Israelites be let go. Once again Pharoah says no. Another plague.

I can only imagine how disappointed Moses was. Not only from the rejection from Pharoah but from the complaining and murmuring that came from the Israelites as they waited to be set free. The weight on Moses had to be enormous, but he went to Pharoah anyway, just as God instructed. And he still encouraged the Israelites that God would lead his people out of bondage.

This constant appearance before Pharoah could have been seen as a failure, but, ultimately, with endurance and patience and the final plague which killed his child, Pharoah indeed let the people go. But what a price he had to pay! The loss of the firstborn of all of Egypt and his son."

At that part, I jumped in saying, "Miss Mazey, where was the peace? Where was the joy during the trial? Every day the Israelites awakened in bondage, subject to the whim of the slave master. Each day the people looked to Moses to deliver them. Each day they waited."

Miss Mazey sighed, turning her hands in her lap. "And yet, in the timing of God, the Israelites were indeed set free. In time they were indeed led on the journey to the promised land. In time.

Now when Pharaoh had let the people go, God did not lead them by the way of the land of the Philistines, even though it was near;

for God said, 'The people might change their minds when they see war and return to Egypt.' Therefore, God led the people around by way of the wilderness to the Red Sea; and the sons of Israel went up in battle formation from the land of Egypt." (Exodus 13.17 – 18)

Even though the people were in battle formation, the battle was the Lord's. He led them. He prepared the way. He guided them and instructed them in the way they were to go. He planned to defeat the enemy and He ultimately did.

Haven't you ever wondered why you have to go through the desert? Why do the circumstances in your life lead you around and around but not directly to your promise or your purpose?

Well, God wants to ensure you are ready to receive the blessings He has for you. You must be prepared and equipped to receive something, or you would throw away what was given to you. You wouldn't value it. You wouldn't recognize that what you have came from God. You wouldn't give Him the glory for your good fortune.

And, If you aren't ready for the battle, if the fight is too hard, you'll give up. You won't value the struggle. You won't learn the lesson from the test. And yes, most struggles are based on a test, a trial by the Lord.

Moses said to the people, 'Do not be afraid; for God has come to test you, and so that the fear of Him may remain with you, so that you may not sin' (Exodus 20.20)."

Miss Mazey let the words sink in and I was glad for the silence. I wondered how the Exodus fits in with my life.

And just when I was trying to put the pieces together Miss Mazey, sensing my thoughts said, "Peace comes in time, at the end of the war, the struggle. Rest and relaxation are rewards for the effort. You're worn out from the seeming endlessness of the battle and it's time to take it down for a while. You'll value peace when you know you have to get back up again, and God has given you the strength to do it. And He said, 'My presence shall go with you, and I will give you rest (Exodus 33.14)."

Enthralled, gaining enlightenment, I said to Miss Mazey, "The end of the battle also reveals the tasks ahead, setting up of camp, taking care of the wounded. There isn't always a bounty to be collected but there is land to be captured, property to be claimed. So, I have to ask myself do I equate this to my life?"

"We aren't always in a physical war, but we are continually in a spiritual one," Miss Mazey said. "The 'land' is your peace, your existence, your way of life, and then there are your relationships. Keeping your mind sharp and focused on the tasks at hand takes effort and timing. You're constantly battling against the effort it takes to keep what you have, to get what you want. And when you have it, you're off to the next conquest. A cycle you'll repeat throughout your life. But I'm here to tell you there is a better way.

Jesus answered, 'Truly, truly, I say to you, unless someone is born of water and the Spirit, he cannot enter the kingdom of God' (John 3.5).

Believe! Trust God to work it all out! Enter His throne room by trusting in His Son. The rest will follow. The Holy Spirit will lead the way. All you need to do is ask Him to."

I thought about scripture and shared it with Miss Mazey. "Jesus said, 'Follow me', He said to the disciples whom he called (Matthew 4.19)."

Miss Mazey, nodding, said, "Yes! Follow Him! He will lead you into that seemingly elusive quality of rest. Isn't it enough to stop and be still? To have joy and happiness is what peace implies. This is the more of it, the rest of it."

"How do you acquire this rest?", I asked.

"Jamie, a sacrifice of your time to spend time with the Lord is what's required. Spending more time with Him than you do with anything and anyone else is the answer. Giving your life to Him with abandon, knowing He will fill it with wonderful things, is part of the journey. Time. Time well spent. This is the journey of peace.

Notice I keep saying 'It's a journey'. Peace is not just something you receive, it's part of what you do. Over time, it becomes a part of who you are and how you go about accomplishing tasks.

Think about this. What do you value? Where is your treasure? 'For where your treasure is, there your heart will be also' (Matthew 6.21, Luke 12.34).

Time spent alone with God is worth more than anything you can possess on earth. It is more valuable than riches. Yet, it is the one thing we can have in abundance, in never-ending supply."

I shared, "I'm challenged to find the time or enough time to spend with God when my job requires so much of my time. That's why I treasure our time together! But I have to tell you, it's a sacrifice as I'm not doing other things that still need to get done. It seems like I never have enough time!"

Miss Mazey shook her head, yes, understanding the challenge. She chimed in, "We always make time for what we want to do and not enough time for what God wants us to do!"

"I can't argue with that," I said.

"What do you strive for?" Miss Mazey said with animation. "And why? What is taking possession of your time such that you can't give any to God? Why does it seem so foreign to you that you should want to give this time to Him? How precious it is to have the attention of the Creator of the Universe?"

Miss Mazey stopped for a moment. She looked at me quizzically and then said, "I want you to take a moment and just contemplate all of those questions for a moment. The Creator of the Universe wants to spend time alone with you! How grand! What a blessing! What a treasure! How amazing is that? He said, 'Do not store up for yourselves treasures on earth, where moth and rust destroy, and where thieves break in and steal. But store up for yourselves treasures in heaven, where neither moth nor rust destroys, and where thieves do not break in or steal' (Matthew 6.19 – 20)

I want you to take a moment and just 'be' with God. Not having anything to do but just to 'be'. It's been a long time since you were to yourself and not being what someone else needed. Right now, here with me, you are just God's child. Ethereally you! You are "extremely delicate and light in a way that seems too perfect for this world" as the definition says. You are ethereal.

Breathe. Take a moment to take in the oneness of who you are."

I closed my eyes and let the warmth of her words and her soothing tone embellish me. In a moment I felt wonderful, beautiful.

As if on cue, Miss Mazey said, "You are beautiful, a delight! You are a wonder of creation! You are marvelously made. God formed you to be His child, His friend, His awesome wonder! 'For You created my innermost parts; You wove me in my mother's womb' He said in Psalm 139.19. You are God's masterpiece. He has created you for splendid things."

I sighed taking in the awesomeness of how King David, inspired by God, describes how we appear to God. Leave it to Miss Mazey to find the right words at the right time.

"What time are you willing to let go of to be with the eternal God of all creation?" Miss Mazey started up again. "What time are you ready to sacrifice to have a moment in His arms, enveloped by His love? Isn't it worth it? Aren't you worth it?"

After a time of silence and with much thought I said, "Well, I ask myself, have I not sacrificed enough love for those who do not know what love truly means? Can't I give true love to the One who formed me?

I sit and watch the clouds form. I watch the gentle falling of a fall leaf. I marvel at the birds of the air and listen as a dog barks in the distance. All of God's creation I see and hear, knowing He created it all. I marvel knowing He made me. The intricacy by which he made each part so masterfully joined. And then to give me the breath by which I live. I am amazed!

"Moments of such quiet are a treasure! Miss Mazey continued. "There is no better time to be had except with someone you love. But even then, to have a moment when you are just you and God is there, and you are one with Him. This treasure cannot be found any other way."

I hum a sigh of contentment. I breathe a sigh of relief and joy. Knowing my Creator in just this moment is pure pleasure. I bask in it! Bathe in it! Let it flow!"

Miss Mazey went on with relish, animated and changing her position, "There is another reality of rest I want to talk about, the Sabbath Rest. This is a rest given by God that includes the provision, an end of work. Don't think of this as retirement but an end to the endless striving and worrying. God will provide. You will live in houses you didn't build. You will eat from farms you didn't plant. You will have clothes you didn't make. This is what the Israelites were supposed to have when they conquered the promised land.

'Therefore, let us fear if, while a promise remains of entering His rest, any one of you may seem to have come short of it. For indeed we have had good news preached to us, just as they have also; but the word they heard did not profit them, because it was not united by faith in those who heard. For we who have believed enter that rest, just as He has said, 'As I swore in My wrath, they shall not enter My rest,' although His works were finished from the foundation of the world' (Hebrews 4.1-3).'

We now have a rest on earth that we can enter when we believe. Won't you enter His rest and secure your peace?"

Because I couldn't argue and had no inspiring words to say, I sat in silence taking it all in. Miss Mazey was content to let me have my thoughts as though she knew I would ruminate on her words for quite some time.

The day seemed to linger on as the sun made its way over the sky. Sunset came with me and Miss Mazey still sitting on the porch, rocking ourselves in peace. There was no rush to go on to do other things. We just let the day go on.

CHAPTER 3
The Path to Peace

I've pondered that it's always clearer how we move forward when we know others are watching. It's so very different when the only one who knows what you are doing is you alone. But the point here is that you are never really alone. God is always watching. God is waiting for you to make the right choices. The question is, will you?

Miss Mazey taught me peace is more than an emotion or an experience. It's a state of being. You must want to be at peace.

There was a time in my life when all I wanted was to be able to be still. No matter what the time of day I couldn't keep still. It was as if everything ganged up on me at once and no matter what I did I couldn't get it together. This went on for months, years. Until finally, I took it all to God, asking Him to calm my nerves and make my life simpler. What I learned is that my life was always simple, I made it complicated trying to be who I was not, trying to accomplish what was not for me to do.

I came by Miss Mazey's house after a long day of work. I wanted to soak up the setting sun and be in a place of quiet peace. Seems we liked the sunset best.

Sitting on the porch and looking over the flower bed was just what I needed. Miss Mazey's house wasn't overly large, but it was comfortable, and being in her presence was always soothing.

She has a swing on the porch and rocking chairs side by side. When I pulled up into the yard, I found her sitting on one of the rockers, her Bible in her lap.

After pleasantries, a big hug, and a smile from her, I asked her, "Miss Mazey, do you ever wonder, is this all there is? And then find yourself creating projects and activities, trying to fill in the void?"

"Oh dear, we all run from one thing to the next," she said. "Always seeking that elusive something that will make us happy. The problem is it's elusive. You'll never find peace until you surrender to it. Not until you really want it!

And most of the time we don't know what peace looks like. We think it's the absence of something but what it is is the fulfillment of everything. When you have peace, you find yourself happy, joyful, and awash with a good feeling all over.

I can imagine this is how the Israelites felt when, after parting, the Red Sea washed over the enemy and the people knew they were safe (Exodus 15.4). I can only imagine what it felt like when the people realized they were now going to move forward toward the promised land. To be free!

You can be free too! Jamie, you don't have to walk in despair, shackled to pain, hurt, and upset. You can let go of the past and walk into the freedom that awaits you on the other side of hope. It's just at the door, knocking. It's Jesus asking you to let Him in."

I sat rocking in the chair taking it all in. After a while, Miss Mazey said, "Stillness of the mind comes when you realize you don't have to be a slave to anything anymore. You can be free and live in that freedom."

Miss Mazey stopped for a moment, picked up some flowers that lay next to her, and began to arrange the flowers in the vase. "Peace is a part of that exercise of freedom. Just knowing you don't have to live a life entangled anymore, you don't have to be bound to a future that has no hope in it, is the freedom that brings peace.

You don't have to be ashamed of the life you lived before you knew Jesus. You can let all that hurt and shame and suffering go. You are washed in the blood of the only sacrifice that could cleanse you from sin and guilt. Jesus. Oh, what a sweet life there is when you give yourself over to His total love. The greatest gift God has for you is love. Peace is the after-effect, a beautiful gift just for you."

I watched as she deftly put the flowers one by one into the vase into an elegant arrangement. Her words were in rhythm with her hands.

"When you think about it truly, you find that life is very simple. You need shelter, transportation, food, clothing, and income for it all. God wants to provide these things for you if you'll let Him. 'For the Gentiles eagerly seek all these things; for your heavenly Father knows that you need all these things' (Matthew 6.32)."

"Miss Mazey, all I've ever wanted was love," I said reflectively. "A companion through life as I travailed and went on the journey."

Miss Mazey replied," God provided me with the love I so desperately needed and wanted. Won't you let Him come into your life more deeply to transform it?"

As if reading my mind Miss Mazey went on, "But you say, 'How will He make me into the person I so desperately want to be but don't know how to be?' God is a giver, a transformer, and a lover of the good because He is love and He is good. All He's ever wanted for you is to live life abundantly, to be the best you could ever be by being His child, HIs daughter.

The journey of Love has many obstacles because you get in the way. Your image of yourself deceives you into believing you can never be enough, you aren't worthy, you'll never make a difference, and no one will ever need you or miss you when you're gone. These are lies! LIES! Don't you ever believe them! 'But in all these things we overwhelmingly conquer through Him who loved us' (Romans 8:37)."

Turning her head to look directly at me, she said, "Don't you know you are a treasure? 'Blessed are the poor in spirit, for theirs is the kingdom of heaven' Matthew 5.3."

"But I feel so broken", I suddenly cried. I was thinking of my divorce and the fact that I was forty-five and single all over again. Even though I had to get out of the relationship because of physical and verbal abuse, it still hurt. Divorce is ripping apart two lives that were meant to be one for a lifetime.

"Healing always starts with brokenness," she said, taking my hand in hers. "Sometimes you hold onto the past for far too long and don't give yourself the grace to let it go. I want you to believe God loves you so much that He will take away all the hurt, all the frustration, all the fear, and all the anxiety. Remember, He said to be anxious for nothing (Philippians 4.6)."

She paused for just a moment and looked deeply into my now weeping eyes. "Letting go of the things that keep you from being free, being centered is what I want you to do. Just know freedom carries with it a bigger weight and has a bigger story. It's the sinfulness you struggle with, the deceit, the lies you tell yourself that keep you bound to the ruler of this world, Satan. He wants you to believe you aren't good enough, can't do well enough, aren't worthy. He's a liar! He wants to steal your life, steal your dreams, and kill your soul.

Jesus said, 'I have come that you might have life and have it more abundantly' John 10.10."

Patting my hand and pulling me up out of the chair and into her arms, she said, "Blessings on blessings, that's what I want for you. And you can have them if you trust the Lord and lean not to your own understanding Proverbs 3.5.

I know it's hard trusting God. You're scared. Scared He won't do for you what His Word says He will because you don't think you deserve it. Then, because you can't see Him face to face, you wonder if He's even there. The key is you have to learn to see Him in all of creation for He is the Creator, the one who created you. You must know He is listening and watching all the time. He knows your every thought and every move."

Turning my attention to the trees in the yard, she continued, "Look at a leaf and marvel that no two leaves on a tree are alike. God took time to intricately put together all of that and made it all unique, giving the seed the power to reproduce itself uniquely. You are no different! The seed makes a replica of itself to produce offspring. So, He formed you in your mother's womb (Jeremiah 1.5) and wants you to know Him intimately. That relationship is the secret, the key that unlocks the door to trusting Him.

Get to know God and He will give you peace. Jesus said, 'Peace, I leave you. My peace I give to you; not as the world gives, do I give to you. Do not let your hearts be troubled, not fearful' John 14.27. God has a plan for you, a plan to prosper you and to give you a future. Jeremiah 29.11. Believe in Him and accept the eternal life He gives."

Patting my arm she said, "God wants nothing but good things for you, but do you want what He has to give? Why do you always think there is a price to pay when God gives freely to those who seek Him? You have yet to learn what it means to believe in Him, to trust in Him."

Miss Mazey pulled me gently to her and held my hands in hers. She said looking deeply into my eyes, "Let God talk to you. You can listen if you're willing. He wants to tell you stories of love, hope, goodness, and kindness. He wants to give you desires that agree with the plans He has for you. He wants to share all the love He has for you that led Him to create a world just for you. If you'll let Him."

I hugged her again tightly! I didn't want to let go.

Wiping my eyes, we sat again in the rocking chairs. Miss Mazey took my hands in hers and for a while, all was right with the world.

I knew in time I'd have to go home but didn't want to. Even though it was getting late I felt being on the porch with this beautiful woman was all I wanted to do. Alas, I knew I had to prepare for the next day.

After a long while we said pleasantries and I got in the car to leave. I went home feeling freer than I ever had. I began to think there was something more to this walk with Jesus than I had ever thought. Through Miss Mazey, the Holy Spirit was convicting me to seek Him out, to go deeper in my walk with Him. I wanted what God had to give me. I wanted the peace Miss Mazey had. I wanted to be free!

CHAPTER 4
Patience

A week had passed since my last visit with Miss Mazey. I got busy with work and things I needed to do around the apartment. I was getting frustrated with all the things I had to do. Seemed like people were moving at a snail's pace when I needed them to move quickly. I wanted them to move quickly is more like it.

I called Miss Mazey frustrated and needing to vent. She let me go on for a while and then she said, "Jamie, have patience. A fitting word for what we so often lack. We often don't want to experience the drama that goes along with having patience. Yet God wants us to know this experience and to have it in abundance. God's word says, 'So, as those who have been chosen of God, holy and beloved, put on a heart of compassion, kindness, humility, gentleness, and patience' (Colossians 3.12)."

"Miss Mazey, what does all that mean in simple terms? I have to put up with a whole bunch of mess to please God?" I said angrily. "I am so angry at life for giving me so many burdens, and so much trouble. I wanted to believe God would see me through everything, that these were just passing troubles, but I'm having a hard time believing when the problems seem to just keep coming!"

Miss Mazey reflected, "We must endure all things. Love through all things. Hope for all things. Knowing that the God of all is with us and for us and in us, changing all that we are by His most perfect love.

Be guided by His awesome lovingkindness, enduring for a season all the ineffable sins of man against you, being patient for His love to abound and wash away the sins. God takes no pleasure in man's inherent sinfulness and does not want you to endure it either. But He knows we have fallen and must contend with one another while He yet molds us into the perfect image of His Son. So, we patiently wait."

I could feel Miss Mazey looking at me even though we were on the phone. Her words were penetrating my stony, angry heart.

Miss Mazey gave a reflective sigh and continued, "Love endures and has not the desire to harm or hurt. Love overcomes, it conquers, and it leads you away from things that may do you harm. Love brings patience. To be free, you must know love, patience, happiness, prosperity, and joy. Patience helps you deal with the changes happening all around you and with the changes happening to you. Patience helps you to endure challenges as they come.

We watch as the change happens to each of us as we grow in love. Love opens doors to everlasting peace. Love is God and God is love. There is no other way to please Him than that you love your brother, your sister."

"Miss Mazey, I have been so hurt by people who say they love me. I don't know if I can open myself up to loving anyone again," I bemoaned.

"It doesn't matter how hurt you may have been or may be," she shared patiently. "Let go of the pain that seeks to keep you bound and cause you to sin. Let go of the desire to harm another because you feel pain. Let go of it all! Be free! Be content with what you have and let God prosper you in the spirit and your nature.

It doesn't take much to allow the Holy Spirit to transform your life. It only takes a willing heart and an open mind. Allow God to soften your hardened heart. Allow Him to set you free, totally free from the shackles which enslave you to sin and doubt, fear, and hurt. You'll have victory when you let love conquer your ailing heart and bring you to the only one who can heal it."

"How can I let go of the pain that has comforted me for so long?" I cried.

"The past doesn't have to hold you captive anymore. You don't have to let the hurts and the pains overshadow the love that God has for you. Let go and be free!

I keep telling you to be free, yet you probably wonder how you can be free when you feel so many negative things have happened in your life. I tell you it is God that can heal you. Through His son, Jesus, you can live afresh, you can be healed, born again liberated. All you have to do is have faith and believe."

She continued after a moment's pause. "You see, the two go hand in hand: faith and belief. It's not enough to just believe, but you must have faith to move mountains. It only takes a little faith to transform the human heart from stone to a living, beating, pliant muscle. And to have faith you have to know that God can do 'exceedingly, abundantly above all that you can ask or think, according to the power that works in us' (Ephesians 3.20, NKJV). How splendid are His grace and His mercy!"

I stayed quiet and Miss Mazey took advantage of it. "I have a chore for you to do, something that will take time to conquer. I would ask that you mind the way you do things, being conscious of your fellow man and keeper of the love of God in your life. Profess your love of Jesus in ways that don't seem marvelous or special, but which can transform a life; give with your whole heart to those who have little. Do it in secret with no fanfare, seeking no glory. Paul said, 'Be kind to one another, just as we are told to be', Ephesians 4.32. Don't allow hate to have room in your heart. Open your heart to Jesus, the one who can bring you peace.

Miss Mazey, I whined. "I don't think I'm ready for one more new thing to do!"

Continuing right along she said, "I say this is a chore because at first, you may not want to do it. You may not have it in you to give to the unfortunate. But over time, as you see the pleasure your gifts bring to others, you will seek to do this more often for the sheer pleasure it gives you on the inside. In time, you'll love giving. You'll understand that giving leads to a happy heart and a happy heart has the patience to endure the actions of others, even when they are contrary to joy and peace."

"Miss Mazey, I don't know if I have the heart for all this," I whined again.

Miss Mazey kept right on talking as though she hadn't heard me at all. "You'll have much to say to others about the life God is giving you when you have a love for one another. You'll want to do things that make God glad, things that are in His will. You won't want to grieve the Holy Spirit. You'll seek to do things that lighten your heart and bring you peace. In time, you'll teach others this blessed gift and they will be happier too. The more you give the more you'll want to give, and others will want to be around you because you are happier, freer, and more peaceful."

"Ok," I said wearily. I wasn't sure I wanted to do what Miss Mazey said but I knew if I tried, I would have the results she informed me of. I just shook my head.

"Patience has many sides and many variables," she continued.

"You don't have to do any one thing, but all things bring peace and joy to those around you. Soon, you'll discover a passion for being peaceful and a joy that transcends the natural things of the world."

"What should I give?" I asked even though I still wasn't quite resolved to do what Miss Mazey was telling me to do but I didn't want to argue with her. There just was no reason to.

"Socks, gloves, a pair of shoes, a meal, a hug, and yes, money are all types of things you can give. But consider giving time, just being with another, and talking about the glory of God in your life. This is the ultimate gift you can give! Don't stress how you do it. Just do it!

You'll discover you aren't so upset when people do things that are not nice or are challenging. You won't get angry so much when others don't agree with your way of doing things. You won't be controlling or manipulative because compassion will rule your heart. You'll understand the prosperity of the soul is greater than monetary rewards. I say all these things because they happened to me. I can testify that the reward for being conscious of how you treat others and taking the time to let go of the need to control circumstances and situations leads to such a life of peace and prosperity that cannot be measured. Patience and giving play such a major part in developing peace; you'll be amazed at how full your life is when you discover its riches."

"Thank you, Miss Mazey," I said. I was not quite convinced, but she did give me plenty to think about. I wondered how giving to others was going to make me feel better, but I trusted her wisdom. I'd seen time and time again how the Lord blessed what she shared with me and with others. I resolved I must have hope!

CHAPTER 5
Time to Give

On a balmy summer day, I came over to Miss Mazey's to help weed the backyard flower garden. Why in the world we picked such a hot day I'll never know! But whenever Miss Mazey got it in her head to do a thing, that's what we did. It didn't matter that it was 80 degrees, with only the occasional breeze to cool us off. It was weeding time!

Seemed like every bug wanted to find its way to visit me. Maybe it was because of the water from the nearby lake. Maybe it was because of my lotion. I don't know but I was getting eaten up by mosquitos and annoyed by flies.

Out of the blue Miss Mazey said, "Jamie, did you find the time to give?"

I answered her with a soft voice, "Well, I have to tell you, Miss Mazey, I wasn't convinced but after muddling through it, yes, I did. I decided to give away some clothes I hadn't worn in a long time to the church. Then I decided to donate to the food pantry in town."

"How did it make you feel?" She asked.

"Well, at first, I did it because you suggested I should not because I felt any gumption to do it. I've got to tell you that after I gave away the clothes, I felt better about myself. I didn't feel so heavy when I thought about who might be blessed with them. That made me want to give to the food pantry because I thought about all those people who didn't have enough to eat. It all made me want to do more! Then I thought I should do more. I could certainly afford to. God has blessed me so much! For just a moment I felt selfish for not having done this long ago. But then I thought it's better to start giving than not to."

"Giving prospers the soul," she intoned. "It takes time to prosper the soul, and time to understand the riches that come with doing what God says. 'Give and it shall be given to you.' It takes time to understand money is not the only way God prospers His children. You've got to want to prosper to be truly prosperous. It takes fortitude, determination, and drive. It takes understanding you're not in control of everything. You are not in control of much at all except your response to your surroundings and circumstances you encounter."

Miss Mazey dug into a particularly stubborn patch of weeds with relish. "'In the day of prosperity be happy, but in the day of adversity consider— God has made the one as well as the other so that man will not discover anything that will be after him' Ecclesiastes 7:14".

"Miss Mazey, what's the most important lesson on prosperity?" I asked wiping the sweat off my brow. Seemed Miss Mazey had changed the focus of the conversation, but I was indeed intrigued.

"You determine how you will respond to others, to what they do," she said sitting on the back of her legs. "Character develops and you learn not to respond to everything. Sometimes no response is the best response. Sometimes not being first or number one is better. It is indeed better to serve. The joy on the face of the one being served is so much greater, so far better."

After a while, Miss Mazey stopped weeding and got up to stretch. With the change in position, she changed the topic.

"God loves you with a love you cannot contain, cannot measure. Love prospers the soul and makes one rich in blessings. Love overflowing is even better, for it waters the soul of the receiver and energizes them, quickening the spirit. What wouldn't you do for Love? What haven't you done for love?"

"I don't know Miss Mazey. Doesn't seem like love has found me yet," I said still digging and scraping the weeds.

"Sometimes we think we have to do something to be seen and heard and loved," she said. "Nope. The reality is in being loving and kind and caring to others, knowing God will give us the love we need in return. You don't have to strive for identity in love, you only need to trust God for the love you need. Let's finish up for the day. It's too hot to do any more work in this yard. I think we made really good progress for today."

I arose from my knees and grabbed our few utensils. We headed back to the house.

Miss Mazey got the hose and turned on the water to rinse off the utensils and cool us both off as we washed off some of the dirt from our arms and hands. We hadn't worn gloves as Miss Mazey liked to feel the dirt on her hands. She said it made her feel more in touch with nature.

Putting the hose away Miss Mazey continued her thoughts. "Love brings peace and joy and happiness. Love ends stress and strife. Love is an action, more than just a feeling. Love endures and hopes and promises. Love is giving. Love is caring. Love does not provoke. 'Love is patient, love is kind and is not jealous; love does not brag and is not arrogant' 1 Corinthians 13:4. Love produces evidence of its existence in the lives of those who share it. 'But the fruit of the Spirit is love, joy, peace, patience, kindness, goodness, faithfulness, gentleness, self-control; against such things, there is no law' Galatians 5:22-23. No one can say they have not loved when Love is God and God is all around us."

We each took a chair on the porch. Miss Mazey poured us each some lemonade from a pitcher prepared earlier.

"By His mercy, God gave us life through His Son, Jesus Christ," she continued after taking a sip of the lemonade. "By His love, He invites us all to be a part of His family and to have eternal life with Him. Love caused Him to ensure mankind would continue even when we sinned against Him. It caused Him to send Adam and Eve away so that they would not eat of the Tree of Life and remain in their fallen state away from God for eternity.

God showed His love even though man disobeyed. 'Then the Lord God said, 'Behold, the man has become like one of Us, knowing good and evil; and now, he might stretch out his hand, and take also from the tree of life, and eat, and live forever'— therefore the Lord God sent him out from the garden of Eden, to cultivate the ground from which he was taken. So, He drove the man out, and at the east of the garden of Eden He stationed the cherubim and the flaming sword which turned every direction to guard the way to the tree of life.' Genesis 3.22 -24"

We each drank our lemonade and looked out over the garden for a while. Listening to the song of the birds chirping and the grasshoppers rubbing their wings soothed my soul and seemed to make Miss Mazey reflective.

"Peace is an outpouring of love," She said looking out over the garden. Peace is a state of being known to those who have love. Love makes room for peace to come and brings happiness and joy with it. Love doesn't cost a thing; it has already paid the price for you."

"Who paid the price for me?" I asked softly.

"Jesus gave you everlasting love and peace," Miss Mazey said.

"He said, 'My peace I give to you' (John 14.27). Embrace what the Lord has to give you. Be content with what you have and know that He has given you eternal life. He professed he wanted you to have life and to have life abundantly, John 10.10. Don't settle for less than He has to offer you through His promises. Know that He is with you and will never leave you. He promised, 'I am with you always even to the end of the age', Matthew 28.20."

Turning to look at me, Miss Mazey asked, "Don't you know you are loved beyond measure? Don't you know the God of the universe loves you so much He's willing to wait for you to be His, waiting until you come around to an understanding of who He is? But know there will come a time when you have to choose whether you will be His or not, whether you will live or die (Deuteronomy 30.19)."

Not knowing what to say I didn't answer. Sitting on the porch and sipping the lemonade gave me a moment of peace. I thought deeply about what Miss Mazey was saying, marveling at her depth of thought. I didn't seem to notice the bugs anymore. I marveled at her resilience.

Full of love I leaned over and took her hand in mine. She just looked at me with a smile and patted my hand. We spent a moment smiling at each other looking out over the garden.

Eventually, I said, "I want more Miss Mazey. I want that peace and love you talk about. I know Jesus is my Savior but what else do I have to do?"

"You say you've accepted Jesus as your Savior, but you didn't say He is the Lord of your life. You have to let Him take over and obey Him as your Lord, the one you answer to and follow. I take it because you say He is your Savior, you asked Him to forgive you of your sins?"

"Yes," I replied.

"Then do this one thing and ask Him to be the Lord of your life. Let God take control. Tell the Lord Jesus you surrender to His will."

"I want to do that," I said. "Tell me how."

Miss Mazey took my hand in hers and we both closed our eyes. She said, "Say this with me. Lord Jesus, come into my heart as My Lord, God, and King. Make room for me in your kingdom. I surrender my will to yours. I surrender all that I am and all that I have to you."

I bowed my head and repeated what Miss Mazy said. Doing so, I felt free. Emotionally I had joy. I knew in my heart that God had heard me, and Jesus was now in control. That brought comfort to my soul.

"Thank you, Miss Mazey!"

Miss Mazey smiled and shook my hand, holding onto it for a while. I didn't know what would happen next, but I sensed I would be able to get through it. I knew I wasn't alone, and Jesus had my life in His hands.

CHAPTER 6

Finding Hope In Love

A few days later Miss Mazey called me. She said the Spirit put me in her heart and she wanted to see how I was doing.

I had had a rough few days and was tired and cranky. I shared I didn't know how I was going to get through the rest of the week with the projects I had to complete being so difficult. The job stresses were really getting to me; impending deadlines, scope creep, and cost overruns were taking their toll. I shared my troubles with her.

"Jamie, it sounds like you lost your hope," Miss Mazey said. "It takes peace to endure the trials and tribulations of life. The offerings of hope and peace bring an everlasting solace that stays with you when life's difficulties overtake you. Staying strong to the end is a hope we are given so that we may endure all hardships that may come. Hope never fails."

"Miss Mazey, I don't know how we're going to get through these next couple of days. The pressure is great, and the team is losing momentum."

"Well, finding true love in the one who is Love is a form of hope. Trusting and believing in the Lord brings with it an everlasting promise that He will 'guide you with his eye upon you and show you the best pathway for your life' Psalm 32.8. It is by hope, coupled with faith, that we ensure we can find peace through any situation."

I sighed. I knew she was right, but I couldn't figure out how to apply the lesson to the situation. I took a deep breath.

As on cue Miss Mazey said, "These three, faith, hope, and love, provide the foundation on which we can stand firm in the knowledge of Him who is our Lord, Jesus Christ. It doesn't matter how hard times may get; we know that in Him we are assured we will get through it. The Psalmist said, 'Be strong and let your heart take courage, all you who hope in the Lord' Psalm 31:24. Stop striving and let love overtake your heart. Believe in the one who formed you and be at peace. It will all work out. Trust God! He will see you through."

"How do we let go when everything around us seems to be falling apart?" I asked her.

"Don't give in to despair, knowing that God has a plan for you. A plan to prosper you. God said, 'For I know the plans that I have for you,' declares the Lord, 'plans for welfare and not for calamity to give you a future and a hope' Jeremiah 29.11. Hold on by faith. I'm going to let you think about that for a while. You be encouraged. It will all work out."

I marveled at how quickly Miss Mazey got right to the point and gave me a strong word of wisdom to hold onto and ponder. As I hung up the phone, I thought about how odd it was that God led Miss Mazey to call me right at that moment and to give me a word that would make me think about what I was doing and what God was doing in my life.

What plans did God have for me? How was He going to ensure my welfare and prevent calamities in my life? Seemed like everywhere

I turned I was faced with bad news or people fussing. Nothing I did seemed good enough at work. I was stressed out, trying to figure out what to do. I was afraid for my job. We were running late on a project, and I was the project manager. My boss and his boss wanted me to have answers, and frankly, I didn't have any.

What do you do when everything seems to be falling apart and peace is far away?

I went to bed that night praying God would give me insight into how to solve the problems at work. I asked Him to lead me and to help me find peace.

The next day I went to work, and it seemed like everything came at me at once. Somehow though, I felt calm, I had answers. I took on each question with the knowledge I knew came from God. The day wasn't peaceful, but I was.

When I got home that night, I called Miss Mazey and shared the news of what God had done for me, that even though the day was hard like all the rest, I had a sense of knowledge from God that made everything all right.

"Knowing God is the problem solver takes all the stress away," Miss Mazey said. "Just rely on Him and He will give you what you need. God is the provider, the healer, and your strength. He is all you'll ever need. God will encourage you. He will provide you with the knowledge and understanding you need to be able to have that blessed assurance that everything will work out. Christ is within you, helping you, filling you with understanding and knowledge to get done what needs to be done. All you ever have to do is ask Him for His help. 'Ask, and it will be given to you; seek, and you will find; knock, and it will be opened to you' Matthew 7.7."

"Everything seemed to fit today. I had the knowledge to answer tough questions and remained calm all day!" I said with elation and wonder.

Miss Mazey took it all in as though this was all normal to her. She said with her even tone, "It doesn't matter what experiences you've had today, doesn't matter what may come tomorrow. Live your life for today and let tomorrow take care of itself. You can only do one good thing at a time. We are not meant to carry the burden of hardship. We aren't meant to solve every problem by ourselves. It takes others, brothers, and sisters. Ultimately, it takes God leading and guiding you, showing you the right pathway to take for your life. He said, 'I will instruct you and teach you in the way which you should go; I will counsel you with My eye upon you' Psalm 32.8."

Pondering out loud I said, "Does it ever feel like there's a war going on in your life and you're the victim, a casualty of other people's aggression? Does it ever feel like everything is against you and there is no way out, no hope for better days?"

"The devil is a liar!" Miss Mazey said resolutely. "The problem is most of us don't know that!"

"How do you fight an enemy you can't see? How do you hold on against antagonistic people, people making life difficult?" I sighed.

"We hold onto our faith! That's the solution!" Miss Mazey intoned. "You don't have to see him to know the devil is real. God tells us to stand and hold up our shield of faith against his fiery darts. The weapons of our warfare are not carnal or of the flesh. We must fight that devil with God's Word and hold onto the Truth!"

Shaking my head in agreement I said, "I hear you, Miss Mazey! It's just that at times it seems nothing works."

"Don't worry about that," She said. "That's when your faith kicks in and you pray to God for what you need. Remember he said to acknowledge Him in all your ways, and He will give you the strength and the courage you need for the situation."

"I am sorely trying but it's not easy," I sighed.

"Wasn't meant to be. Jesus told us that in this life we will have tribulation. That means we are to be prepared for difficulties in life. But He also said, 'My peace I leave with you. Not as of this world." He tells us He overcame this world. So, we have to hold onto Him and His unchanging hand. We have to fight when we are weary knowing from where our help comes from. Remember, the battle is the Lords."

"I will hold on, Miss Mazey," I said half-heartedly.

"You do that!" She reminded me.

We hung up after a while. I sat on the couch staring out the window hoping and praying, wanting things to work out for my good as Miss Mazey always says.

The next day I went to work with a sense of hope but no particular plan. I decided I'd take each day as it came.

Things got better after a while but there always seemed to be an undercurrent of turmoil and strife lurking ahead.

I answered questions from my boss with relative calm. I had answers, praise the Lord. But no matter how many answers I had or how much work I did, there was that undercurrent of turmoil. I could sense it. I dreaded being at work.

I remembered Miss Mazey said "You can't live your life in dread and fear. Fear is the enemy. God did not give us a spirit of fear. 'For God has not given us a spirit of timidity, but of power and love and discipline" 2 Timothy 1:7.

Too bad that in the moment fear is the aggressor and we forget who we are and whose we are. Miss Mazey says, "You are bought and paid for with the blood of the Lamb. You are not your own."

I went about my days with one foot in dread and the other in calm. I thought this is no way to live! You cannot have one foot in the world and one foot in the kingdom of God.

I decided to call Miss Mazey when I got home from work. After pleasantries, I dove right in.

"Miss Mazey, I can't seem to get out of despair. Nothing I'm doing seems to be enough. I'm always challenged with more, with the next task. I don't get a kind word; I get more work."

"Jamie, breathe and trust God. He never said we wouldn't have tribulations. He did say that He would see you through them. In John 16.33 Jesus says, 'These things I have spoken to you, so that in Me you may have peace. In the world you have tribulation but take courage; I have overcome the world.' Jesus knew there would be dark times, times when things would be hard. Take comfort that He, being greater than Satan and every trial you may come against, has given you comfort. He said, 'Peace I leave with you; My peace I give to you; not as the world gives do I give to you. Do not let your heart be troubled, nor let it be fearful 'John 14.27."

I took a breath. Then another. Suddenly, everything just seemed to make more sense. People were being themselves; scared, demanding. I didn't need to join them in their fear. I didn't need to look for accolades or a pat on the back. I just needed to do the tasks at hand and keep moving forward.

We don't often think about what the other person is going through or the demands that may be being placed on them to produce and succeed. I didn't think about the pressures my boss and his supervisor were under to move the project forward and to produce the desired result which was a satisfied customer with a working product that we created.

I stopped and thought about all the work the team had taken on. All the late nights and long hours. I remembered I wasn't the only one doing work that just seemed never-ending. Everyone on the team was under tremendous stress to perform higher than we thought we could.

"Miss Mazey, how do you point me in the right direction every time?" I said shaking my head in wonder.

Miss Mazey laughed. "It's not me, it's God ordering your steps! Rest in Him! Everything is going to be alright!"

I signed off with "Yes Ma'am". I thought about the wonderful and mysterious way God always seemed to provide the right answer just when I needed it most. Miss Mazey is surely a wonder!

Having faith in God and knowing His word go hand in hand. In times of deepest stress, it's the knowledge of Him and His word that gets you over the difficulties that come. Life is a series of winds and twists in the road, but the ultimate destination is the Kingdom of God in eternity. It doesn't matter how many bumps we incur along the way. What matters is knowing God will see us through to the other side of the problem. I took comfort in the remembrance of this.

I went to work the next day with a satisfied smile knowing that no matter the trials I might face or how difficult the day might be, God was still in control, and I would get through it all. I had an assurance that everything would be all right. I was starting to trust God in new ways.

CHAPTER 7

There is Time for Everything

Time. There never seems to be enough. We're always in a rush, always trying to cram everything into the time we have when we're not at work. Shopping. Cleaning. Cooking. Traveling back and forth to work. Staying up late to get in that last thing. There just doesn't seem to be a way to do all the things we need to do on a given day.

God took me on a journey to give me an understanding of time. "Jamie, there is an appointed time for everything. And there is a time for every event under heaven" Ecclesiastes 3.1. I had to slow down to speed up. Let me explain.

Over a day there are only 24 hours. Within this time there is sleeping and waking, bathing, and dressing, traveling to work, working, eating, and returning home. Once we return home there is eating and relaxing or doing a task, preparing for bed, and sleeping. Somewhere in there we also need to exercise.

In the timeframe of returning home and preparing for bed, we tend to try to cram in as much as possible. The problem is that when we do that, we don't take into consideration how tired we already are and the amount of sleep we need to be refreshed the next day.

God showed me I need eight hours of peaceful sleep to function optimally. I need to organize my time such that I can complete one task. If I complete one task I can then determine if I have enough time to complete the next task before I get tired. I learned that when I am tired, I don't do things as well as I could. I miss steps, take shortcuts, and risks I would not normally take, just to get it done. Then I'm faced with having to start the task over because I didn't do it right the first time.

Another eye-opener is that you need to let God plan your day. Each day indeed takes care of itself.

At the start of the workday, I review tasks that need to get done and determine which one or two I can do to complete. Then I determine who I need to help me and check their availability. This is done between scheduled meetings and meals or snacks.

When I get home, I give myself 45 minutes to sit still. I use this time to think about a meal and give myself a moment to be available to anyone else that comes to mind or that calls or visits. I don't have to rush to do the next thing.

Through Miss Mazey, God revealed it's better to go slow than to move quickly. A slower pace leads you to do things only once and well the first time. She'd remind me," The tortoise wins the race, not the hare. There are no shortcuts to excellence."

Driving home from work I decided to do a little grocery shopping. It was the beginning of fall, and I noticed the leaves were starting to change colors on the trees.

How had I missed that on the way to work? Rushing, distracted, focused on the traffic as usual. I took a pause, rolled down the driver's window, and took a deep breath. How amazing the smell of green grass and fall foliage was! I made a vow to myself that I would take a moment every day to "stop and smell the roses".

Challenges. How we choose to handle situations determines our victory or defeat with people. No matter how disturbing a person's behavior we can choose to rise above the situation and put our best foot forward. I learned this the hard way.

There is a saying, "foot in mouth disease". I've suffered from it on many teams, even most recently. Sometimes we just need to take a moment to think about how we're going to respond to another person, what we're going to or not going to say. It can be difficult because we want to immediately tell that person off or "show them". But I know this isn't the right way to go.

When we don't take a moment to compose ourselves, we wind up saying things we regret. Often, chastisement from God follows, not to mention being called out for our behavior. It only takes a moment to change a person's mind about you for the good or the bad.

2 Corinthians 13.11 says, "Finally, brethren, rejoice, be made complete, be comforted, be like-minded, live in peace; and the God of love and peace will be with you."

Courage. "Be strong and let your heart take courage, All you who hope in the Lord" (Psalm 31:24).

It only takes faith as big as a mustard seed to move mountains. Let your heart be strong in the Lord. And again, "Trust in the Lord with all your heart and do not lean on your own understanding. In all your ways acknowledge Him, and He will make your paths straight" (Proverbs 3.5-6). Encourage yourself in the Lord and He will accomplish the tasks He has set for you. You don't have to understand it all, you only have to believe.

I was learning, when you follow the path He has for you, everything works out according to His plans. Your job is to follow Him, trusting that He will make everything plain in time. It sounds easy but it's the hardest thing you will ever face. The uncertainty in the face of hardship gets to you. You wonder if you're doing the right things, going in the right direction. It takes extraordinary faith to do what God tells you to do. Listening is required. You have to spend more time being quiet than talking. And then not talk to everybody. Some are going to have faith, some aren't. You won't know which ones will and which ones won't. You don't need to be discouraged.

My approach to work and life, in general, was getting easier. I began to understand faith takes perseverance and trust. God will require that you go the extra mile even when it feels like you can't go any further. That's when perseverance takes hold, and you begin to believe you can do all things through Christ. You believe he strengthens you. You know He's with you and will never let you down.

I shared these thoughts with Miss Mazey one evening. I had stopped by to share some apples and pears I had gotten from the greengrocer. I knew how much she loved them.

Miss Mazey counseled, "Trusting God gets easier over time. The more you trust Him the more He will do things for you that prove His loyalty and love for you. But it begins with you trusting Him even when the task seems overwhelming. Reading the Word ensures you develop trust as you believe if He did things for all of those who walked with Him in the Bible, He can do it for you too. He says He's no respecter of persons. What He has done for others He'll do for you. But you have to have faith. Nothing happens without it.

I've been walking with God for just about 50 years and God has proven time and time again that I can trust Him. It wasn't always easy, but it was totally worth it every time."

"Miss Mazey, how can I develop that kind of faith?" I asked.

"It takes time and trust and believing God over and over again, Jamie. It takes a listening ear on the inside, from the heart, to know that what you have to do is from God and not from yourself. Selfishness no longer gets in the way because you want to do what God wants you to do, and you do it for the right reasons.

Just after my husband died, I was tested sorely. I had to raise my babies into strong men and women and lead them the best way I knew how. They were teenagers and just coming into adulthood. With five of them to raise, I didn't know if I had the strength to press through, didn't know if they would listen to me without their father backing me up and guiding them. But I trusted in God's divine guidance to give me the answers I needed when I needed them. Sure enough, He came through every time. But trust me when I tell you, life was hard for a while. I had to work and take care of the house, and my children all by myself.

And it was during their rebellious years. That was tough. We were all learning at the same time, and they weren't sure what they believed in. I had to have faith in them and myself. But God helped me persevere, even though I was still growing and leaning on Him extra hard.

I wasn't totally strong in my faith, but I trusted that what God did for the Israelites He'd do for me. I came to understand that the Bible was the infallible word of God. Every word is true, every inference and reference are meant to instruct and lead to ever-increasing faith. The Bible is the best guide to get you through life. Its lessons are as pertinent today as they were hundreds of years ago.

It takes ever-increasing faith to follow God. It takes endurance. Trust and belief grow as you experience more of His grace and love. You have to want God to transform your life.

You have to want His love to move all those things that aren't good for you out of the way. In time you learn His is the best way. You understand what He means when He says, 'I am the Way, the Truth, and the Life', John 14.6. You don't want to live in sin, don't want to go the way of most people who don't know Him. Oh, they try to live good lives, but they just aren't consistent at it—Sometimes they do good and other times they go a different path. Can't help themselves."

Miss Mazey sighed and continued, "What do you have that is so important that you can't do without it? What do you have that God can't give you again if you listen to Him? Put both feet into faith. Don't straddle the fence with one foot in the world and another trying to follow God. It won't work. Jesus said in Revelation 3:16 'Because you are lukewarm, and neither hot nor cold, I will spit you out of My mouth". Trust me when I tell you, you don't want God to turn His back on you. You don't want Him to leave you to your own devices. Christian living gets easier as you learn to obey Him, to trust He has everything under control and wants the very best for you at all times."

"What about the bad things that happen?" I said.

"Understand we live in a fallen world. Bad things are going to happen because man has free will and choice. Sometimes he does good, other times he doesn't. No one forces him to do evil. He chooses to. No one tells him to get behind the wheel drunk. No one tells him to buy guns. No one tells him to be abusive. No one tells him to lash out at others. It's a choice. And yes, sometimes he listens to Satan and does evil things, but for the most part, he's doing evil on his own."

"But God lets it happen!" I exclaimed.

"As I've told you before, God allows man to make his own choices. This too is part of His love. Yes, bad things happen, but I'm sure it hurts God just as much to see the outcomes of man's choices as it does to those who are left to endure the fallout and consequences. Understanding that God loves us helps you deal with the consequences of other people's actions.

God doesn't want murder or rape or abuse or car accidents to befall anyone. God will often talk to the one who's headed for disaster but, unfortunately, they don't always listen. The Lord has said, 'I create the light and make the darkness. I send good times and bad times. I, the Lord, am the one who does these things. (Isaiah 45.7)"

"You have a way of making even the most complicated things easier to understand," I said shaking my head.

"That's only because God has granted me the wisdom to see the Truth. God promises in Isaiah 65.20, 'No longer will babies die when only a few days old. No longer will adults die before they have lived a full life. No longer will people be considered old at one hundred! Only the cursed will die that young!' We have His promise that good people will live long and prosperous lives. We can hold onto His promises. That's what gets me through each day a little stronger, a little less worse for wear."

"Amen!" I said with relish. Miss Mazey nodded her head in agreement, taking one of the pears and biting into it. She smiled exclaiming over how good and sweet the pear was. We sat for a while enjoying the sweet fruit, the setting sun, and each other's company.

CHAPTER 8
Hope through Pain

Later that week I went to a concert at the Appel Room in Lincoln Center, New York. The hall was beautiful! You could see the city in the background of the stage overlooking the park. I had wanted to come there for many years having seen it as a backdrop of my favorite television ministry.

The concert was amazing but halfway through my legs started bothering me from sitting in the chair. By the end of the concert, I was stiff and in pain.

I drove home and when I got there, I went straight to bed. The next morning the pain in my legs had greatly increased. I thought it would pass, prayed about it, and went about my day. As I was working from home, I tried not to think about it.

Later that evening, when I couldn't take it anymore, I went to my cupboard to get some pain medication and found I didn't have any. By that time, I was desperate and in agony. I shook my head at my foolishness and proceeded to drive to the pharmacy. After taking the pills I barely slept but eventually did get a few hours of peace. I was able to get up in peace the next day, the pain had dissipated.

Two days later I was talking to Miss Mazey on the phone during our weekly call and shared this story with her.

At the end of my tale Miss Mazey said, "Jamie, this sounds so much like the children who don't know God or His grace."

"How so?" I asked.

"Well," Miss Mazey started. "Some are in physical and emotional pain that is at times unbearable. It is very real! They take all kinds of drugs and alcohol to soothe the pain away, but they don't go to the One who can eliminate it. Some have the Bible near and won't read it. Others don't read the Bible even though they have one nearby. Others won't go to God because the voice their listening to convinces them God can't or won't do anything about their problem. Still, others won't cry out to God for help. And others are Christians who cry out to God, and it seems He isn't helping them, but they won't go to the Word to gain strength while they wait. The last group are Christians who cry out to God in desperation during a debilitating disease and instead of healing them, God brings them home to Him. The group I love are people who cry out to God for healing, and He hears them and heals them."

"Wow!" I exclaimed. "I never thought of it that way! I'd never really thought about the struggle of people who didn't reach out to God during their suffering. I didn't think about the reasons why they had such a hard time. I know this, the pain I had was really hard to bear and I suffered for lack of a remedy. What I needed was so simple and yet I didn't realize I had run out of the medication I knew would help."

"This is the way most people live their lives. They don't believe they deserve God's help, or they don't seek God's help. The group that is the hardest to understand is the group that does go to God in prayer, and are earnest believers, and yet God does not heal them. In Isaiah 57.1 God said, 'Good people pass away; the godly often die before their time. But no one seems to care or wonder why. No one seems to understand that God is protecting them from the evil to come.' Many people don't know this scripture. It's seldom taught in churches. But it answers the question of why so many people go home to God seemingly early.

Even when we don't understand why we should know that God has a plan for every soul. He doesn't cause disease, but He will have the best solution for each individual. Sometimes, He will use the situation to teach a lesson to the person with the disease and others in their sphere of influence. God is a loving God and will do what is good for every one of us, even if that means death."

"Miss Mazey, that is so amazing!" I said as I shook my head in awe. "So, what is a person who is suffering to do? They won't know which category they fit into."

"For the unbeliever and the believer, it depends on which state they believe they're in. Will they trust God even when everything tells them not to or will they listen to the other voice that tells them God won't help them. In all instances, it takes faith to trust that God will work it all out. Just like your experience, sometimes you don't have what you need because you aren't prepared for what is to come. Other times what you need is not that far away, you just have to seek it."

"What an amazing journey we're on!" I intoned. "One thing is for sure; I won't take for granted how blessed I am and how much others need guidance to seek God in every situation. I won't turn my nose up at the ones who are addicted and afflicted anymore. I have a bit of a better understanding of how cunning the devil is to keep them cast down. I also understand a bit better how others give up hope when they aren't getting the relief they need. I truly believe

I can be a better helper now that I've experienced what it's like to need relief and finding none, fall into despair. My solution was easy. All I had to do was trust God and go to the store. Others may not have it so easy. I certainly won't judge anyone anymore."

Miss Mazey sighed with satisfaction. I could feel her smile, as she said, "And that is the point of your experience. Sometimes we have to go through some uncomfortable or even painful things to get a glimpse of what it's like for someone else. Praise God you got the lesson! Jamie, you're now in a better position to help others who are struggling and don't know where to turn or who are so despondent that it seems God isn't doing anything. Just remember, God is always working for our good. We just don't always know it or understand why He's doing what He's doing! And frankly, we don't have to! God doesn't fit in a box. His thoughts are higher than ours and His ways are so much greater!"

"Thank you so much, Miss Mazey! I often don't understand what God is doing in my life, but I'm grateful He gave you to me to help me grow closer to Him!"

"You are just as much a blessing to me Jamie!" Miss Mazey said. I could feel her warmth and love through the phone and thought what a blessing to have her in my life! Everyone needs someone to guide them on this journey. I'm just grateful God gave her to me!

CHAPTER 9
Who You Are

We don't often get to share our daily lives with those who are truly called by God. It is a great gift! I realize how blessed I've been to have Miss Mazey as my guide on this journey. She's both a mother and a mentor. I was so moved by our friendship that I went over to her house to thank her. I was filled with love.

I had an especially good week at work, having incorporated the lessons Miss Mazey had given me. Over time, my relationships at work blossomed, and the work became easier to do.

Even though we weren't able to change our delivery date with our client, the burden of developing a new software package seemed to lighten up tremendously. Amazingly, my supervisors began thanking me for my hard work and the team relaxed just a bit. I didn't know how long this peace would last but I wanted to share in the hope I now had and to give my appreciation to Miss Mazey for guiding me through the tough times.

At sunset on an especially beautiful fall day, I pulled into Miss Mazey's driveway and once again marveled at the beautiful garden she created. She had planted beautiful fall flowers just a few weeks before and everything looked lovely.

When I got out of the car, I breathed in the scent of all of the flowers and had such peace envelop me. I sighed in joy as I rang her doorbell.

"Hi, Jamie!" Miss Mazey exclaimed as she opened the front door. "How are you? What a pleasure it is to see you!"

"Hello, Miss Mazey! Forgive me for not calling you in advance to let you know I was coming! I was so full of thanks and joy I just drove straight over here after work without thinking to call you!" I peeled with laughter and a smile as I went through the door.

"No worries! Come on in! Rest yourself and tell me all the good things you have to share!"

Walking past the vestibule into the living room I took in the wonderful smell of jasmine Miss Mazey always had in her home. The room was so peaceful with overstuffed chairs and a roomy sofa. I decided to sit in one of the chairs that faced the fireplace. Even though it was too warm to turn it on there was something soothing about the fireplace and all the pictures of her family and friends on the mantle. There was even a picture of me and her we had taken when I first met her.

"You know, I love this room, Miss Mazey! It's so warm and comfortable!"

"Thank you, Jamie! You always say that every time you come here!"

"Well, it's true!"

As she sat in the chair next to me, Miss Mazey smiled and said, "Now tell me what's going on."

"So much has changed!" I began. "Work is going really well even though the deadlines are still the same and it's still intense. Seems everyone has a better attitude all of a sudden."

"That's grace!"

"Well, praise God!" I smiled.

"Yes, indeed! God always has a hand in the change of circumstances in our lives. Few take the time to notice it though. So, I'm glad you did!"

"I couldn't help but notice. Since our last talk and since I began giving more intently everything has shifted to the positive. Or maybe because I'm paying more attention and God is changing me, I'm seeing things in a different light. One thing is for sure, I don't feel as heavy-hearted and I've started smiling more."

"Praise God!" Miss Mazey exclaimed. "You know your coworkers probably sense the change in you and are responding in kind. Everyone loves a cheerful person."

"That is so true! I hadn't thought about it in that way but you're absolutely right! The team seems more relaxed around me. Even my supervisors are behaving differently."

"God's grace! What else?"

"I'm reading the Bible more and getting more comfortable with being quiet. I feel so peaceful."

"Well, that is good news! Most people can't keep still long enough to enjoy the quiet and the peace!"

"That's true." I agreed. "I find I can sit for long periods of time and hear what God is telling me in His Word. The Bible has taken on a whole new meaning for me. God is instructing me every day."

"That is wonderful!" Miss Mazey said joyfully. "I'm so glad! That reminds me, I have something for you." Miss Mazey rose and went to the desk on the other side of the room. When she returned, she had a small box which she handed to me and said, "I think it's time for you to have this."

"Thank you, Miss Mazey!" I said, taking the box from her.

Opening it there was a small gold cross on a gold chain on the inside. "Oh, Miss Mazey! It's beautiful!"

Miss Mazey sat down smiling. "It's time for you to have a reminder of who you are and who you've become. You don't have to wear it. I just wanted you to have it."

Pulling the chain out of the box I said, "Oh, I will definitely put this on! Can you help me?"

Miss Mazey rose from her chair and put the chain around my neck. It fit perfectly!

"I will treasure this beautiful gift! Thank you!" I said gleefully.

"You are very welcome my dear! Now you're probably wondering why I gave this to you now."

I shook my head affirmatively and she continued.

"Just when things are starting to go well that's when the enemy comes along to test your resolve. We need to remind ourselves that we are more than conquerors and that we're overcomers. Remember, the enemy comes to kill, steal and destroy. He has one purpose and to that purpose, he is totally committed. Let this cross be a daily reminder that Jesus paid a price for your salvation, and He is with you all the time. The scripture reminds us 'He will never leave us nor forsake us', He is always with us no matter what. Hold onto that promise."

"Oh, Miss Mazey!" I said, reaching for her hand. "I will remember always. I won't forget the promise or the one who gave me this beautiful gift!"

Miss Mazey smiled and shook my hand in hers. We sat in companionable silence grateful for each other. I knew this was the beginning of a new chapter in our journey.

As if sensing my thoughts Miss Mazey said, "Today is a new day! No matter what the future may bring we have each other, and we have Jesus. Nothing could be better!"

"Amen, Miss Mazy!" I said delighted.

We sat for quite some time talking and laughing. We shared the events of our lives over the past weeks and relished each other's company. Although I didn't know what might lie ahead of me, I knew I had a friend I could rely on, a teacher who would guide me. I was blessed with love and a feeling of peace I could not explain. The beauty was, with Miss Mazey, I didn't have to.